POSTCARDS FROM

AUSTRALIA

POSTCARDS FROM
AUSTRALIA

A PICTORIAL JOURNEY

EDITED BY CHRISSIE GOLDRICK

**Australian
GEOGRAPHIC**

CONTENTS

Previous page: white sands edge into aptly named Turquoise Bay, WA, with Ningaloo Reef visible on the distant horizon. This page: dawn mist cloaks Pyungoorup and Bluff Knoll, two peaks in Stirling Ranges NP, south-west WA.

FOREWORD

IT'S NOT SURPRISING to learn that photography is the fastest growing hobby in Australia. Driven by advances in digital technology, and fuelled by the ever-expanding publishing opportunities offered by the internet, you can capture and share images like never before. At AUSTRALIAN GEOGRAPHIC, photography has been our passion since we launched the journal in 1986. We have been dispatching our finest photographers to Australia's most remote and relatively unexplored regions ever since. Often supplied with the basics of an off-road vehicle, a tent and an open brief, they surprise and delight us with the results of their efforts, which we then use to celebrate the wonders of this great continent through the pages of the journal. We love to share stunning photography with our readers because we recognise the power of images to inspire and encourage – whether it be to get out and see these places for yourself, to get involved in the efforts to preserve our natural beauty under threat, or to aim for the sky in your own photography. In this book we take you on a visual lap of the island continent; a brilliantly hued, whistlestop tour of our six states and two territories captured through the lenses of our talented and intrepid band of photographers. Be inspired.

Chrissie Goldrick
EDITOR-IN-CHIEF, AUSTRALIAN GEOGRAPHIC.

Pictured left: a quiet dawn breaks over the granite cliffs of Whitewater Wall, a popular climbing spot near Coles Bay in Freycinet NP on Tasmania's east coast.

INTRODUCTION

THE ISLAND CONTINENT is a photographer's dream. There are striking landforms to fill the frame. Not to mention a bevy of eye-catching creatures. Most of all, Australia abounds with the image maker's greatest asset – lashings of sharp light.

From dawn's first glimmers at Cape Byron to the last spark at Shark Bay, the sun can shower its rays on our continent for more than 16 hours, lighting up a jaw-dropping diversity of habitats.

As early light seeps into coastal rainforests, it also jags the tops of the Great Divide. In the deserts the raking shadows of daybreak soon vanish with the morning. Out across our wheat belts and grazing country the march towards midday brings a dazzling brightness. Even the deepest, most shadowy of gorges is no match for the probing outback sun at its zenith.

From the massive sandstone escarpments in the tropical north to the jagged basalt peaks of Tassie's Central Highlands, the land's age-worn facets are etched for all to see. Time has been the artist at work. Across the continent there are surfaces that have been scoured, doused and baked – some for more than 100 million years. To travel this terrain is to be tutored in the language of light – whether you wield a camera or peer from under the brim of a floppy hat.

Australians have an eye for expanse. Our largest capital, Sydney, perches on the edge of a dramatic harbour cradled within a fortress of sandstone and bush. All our cities have this raw outer edge – a feeling of wildness on the doorstep. This immensity breeds a certain rueful patience and humility. At times, the terrain can seem slow to change. Our seasons often stall and falter. There's precious little of the old-world ideal of an ordered landscape. But we do have space to burn. A beachfront vista of open ocean is but an analogue for the gaping vastness of the inland. It may be daunting but this imperious wildness holds a promise – the freedom to explore. For generations, families have loaded the wagon, hooked up the van and taken off.

These trips are often less about a fixed itinerary than embracing the ethos of wanderlust and making-do. In this brand of travel the spirit of DIY discovery lives on. Landforms and seasons set the tempo. Uncluttered spaces teach us to wait and look for details. Slowly but surely, Australians are learning to read the signposts that have always been there, showing the way.

With this knowledge comes an understanding that our continent has never truly been empty. As home to the world's oldest continuous culture, every corner of Australia lives as a place renewed by storytelling and art. We share a land that shines with the gifts of journey-making.

Pictured right: late afternoon light sets Uluru ablaze with fiery hues.

NEW SOUTH WALES AND THE AUSTRALIAN CAPITAL TERRITORY

NEW SOUTH WALES is an amazing place, as diverse as it is beautiful. From the subtropical climes of the far north coast, which nurtures an emerald tangle of World Heritage-listed rainforest, to the snow-dusted peaks of Mt Kosciuszko and the red-earth moonscapes of the outback, the state is a wonderful amalgam of plants, animals, natural landscapes, and indigenous and European heritage. Marry that with Sydney, one of the world's most recognisable cities – with its glittering harbour, sun-soaked beaches, iconic bridge and 'sailing' Opera House – and it's near perfect. In the southern half of the state, NSW encircles the little territory that's home to the nation's well-ordered capital, Canberra.

New South Wales invites exploration. Inland from the state's stretch of coastline there's richness aplenty to discover. Hundreds of walking trails wend through the incomparable Blue Mountains region, which protects soaring escarpments, majestic waterfalls, eucalypt-lined gorges and babbling rivers. To the south, the Snowy Mountains are a year-round playground of winter snow and summer hiking.

Country NSW is renowned for its rich agricultural lands, sprawling plains and inspiring landscapes. Further west, the outback is a mix of vast national parks, idiosyncratic towns, enduring Aboriginal heritage and mesmerising red desert.

Classic Aussie surf adventures, complete with the perfect barrel wave, endless beaches and a laid-back lifestyle, are just some of the attractions of the state's north coast.

The south coast's natural treasures include more than 30 national and marine parks, the latter inhabited by an astounding array of wildlife – from Australian fur seals and colour-changing cuttlefish to dolphins and migratory whales.

AROUND THE STATE AND THE TERRITORY

BATHED IN SUNSHINE, the spectacular harbour city of Sydney is a visual feast – azure water, golden sands and lush pockets of bush housing some of the nation's most beautiful national parks. From the iconic sails of the Sydney Opera House and the 'coathanger' bridge to the world-renowned crescent beaches of Bondi and Manly, Sydney shines.

An astounding landscape on Sydney's back doorstep, the Blue Mountains' ripples and folds protect a world of golden sandstone cliffs, cascading waterfalls, lush gullies and unique wildlife – all veiled by a blue eucalypt-oil haze.

A sublime mix of ancient palms, unique wildlife, wild waterfalls and spent volcanoes, the Gondwana Rainforests of Australia stretch from Barrington Tops to south-eastern Queensland and are part of the most extensive area of subtropical rainforest in the world. Identified in 2011 as one of the world's biodiversity hotspots, the eastern forests region has over 8000 plant species, more than 2000 of which are found nowhere else.

The ACT is also a haven for wildlife – including threatened species such as the brush-tailed rock-wallaby and corroboree frog – and boasts a rich indigenous heritage – more than 20,000 years of human occupation.

Canberra itself is defined by the impressive spire of Black Mountain Tower, the iconic pyramid of Parliament House and the serene waters of Lake Burley Griffin. Completed in 1963, the lake is a magnet for locals who picnic on its grassy foreshore, walk and cycle along its pathways, or swim, row, sail, windsurf, canoe, kayak and fish in its cool depths.

Nationally significant buildings, including the National Museum, National Gallery, National Library and the High Court of Australia, line its banks, as do cafes and restaurants.

The state's alpine country is a wonderland throughout the year. Iced in winter, it's a playground for snow-sport enthusiasts. During spring and summer wildflowers bloom and bushwalkers follow walking tracks that wind through snow gum stands to historic mountain huts built by tough-as-nails high-country cattlemen. Under a blanket of blue sky, summer fishermen tempt trout in the region's streams, while autumn delivers cooler evenings enjoyed around a campfire and beneath an inky sky shining with stars.

From the glistening coast to the towering plateaus and escarpments of the Great Dividing Range, the eastern flank of NSW is spectacular. The ocean is as tempting and blue as a bucketful of sapphires scattered beside golden sand, and the national parks and state forests run with mountain-born rivers and coastal estuaries. In the state's northern reaches, Byron Bay is a magnet for wave riders, beach lovers and alternative lifestylers. Cape Byron, the easternmost tip of mainland Australia, offers 180° panoramic views north, south and east across a seemingly endless ocean punctuated by migrating whales and crest-surfing dolphins, views repeated down the coastline, south from Coffs Harbour, past Crescent Head and beyond.

On the south coast, pearly sands, sheltered beaches and secluded camping areas spoil all who take the time to explore. Australia's oldest national park, the Royal National Park, hugs the coastline south of Sydney and combines magnificent sandstone cliffs with stunning ocean vistas.

From its expansive gibber plains and sun-burned claypans, to its lunar landscape and river red gum-lined waterways, outback NSW is rugged. Stay a while, however, and you'll discover its charms are many: larger-than-life locals; welcoming watering holes; crackling campfires; and sunsets that paint the world the deepest red. Exploring the outback's tough country is always an adventure.

Pictured left: triple icon of the Blue Mountains region, The Three Sisters.

AROUND NEW SOUTH WALES AND THE AUSTRALIAN CAPITAL TERRITORY

Opposite page, clockwise from top left: red siltstone rocks line the coast at Eden; Coogee Surf Club nippers in training under a stormy sky; Bondi Beach; a common ring-tail possum; Sydney Opera House on Sydney Harbour; a pair of musk lorikeets; Manly Beach; Bondi surf lifesavers; a NSW waratah, the state floral emblem. This page, clockwise from top left: Hanging Rock, Blue Mountains NP; Walls of China lunette, Mungo NP; Wallaga Lake, Wallaga Lake NP; a grey-headed flying fox coming to roost in the Royal Botanic Gardens, Sydney; a spotted-tailed quoll; a royal spoonbill; Captain Cook Memorial Fountain, Canberra; Darling Harbour and Sydney's CBD; Hamish Jardine and his mount, Clyde, set off for work on Curry Flat station in the Monaro region of NSW's high country; a shingleback or sleepy lizard defiantly displays its blue tongue.

Waves slam into Bondi ocean baths (opposite), home, since 1929, of the Bondi Icebergs Winter Swimming Club. The Sydney Harbour Bridge (above), aka the 'coathanger', was opened three years later, in 1932, linking Milsons Point, in the foreground, with Dawes Point. Sydney's other main icon, the World Heritage-listed Sydney Opera House, pictured to the left of the bridge, was opened in 1973 by Queen Elizabeth II.

During the day the Sydney Opera House's gleaming white shells (opposite) imitate the billowing spinnakers of sailing boats passing on the harbour, but, as the sun sinks in the west (top), the harbour quietens and the Opera House's interior fills with concert goers. Sydney's tallest structure (bottom) is the 309m-high Sydney Tower, shown in the background. At night the features down by the harbour, such as the 89m-high granite-faced bridge pylons, still provide some of the city's best visual highlights.

BLUE MOUNTAINS

Sydney's wild backyard is the stunning World Heritage-listed Blue Mountains, a rugged landscape of more than 10,000sq.km, with orange cliffs, fern-filled canyons and gorges, rainforest, sandstone plateaus and limestone caves. It's an adventure playground for canyoners, climbers, abseilers, bushwalkers and mountain bikers. Waterfalls, such as the three-tiered Wentworth Falls, plunge off the escarpment to form little rockpools and mini falls (far left). Under ground, the stunning shawls and features of Orient Cave (left) make up some of the many delicate limestone attractions in the Jenolan Caves. By far the most well-known natural feature, however, is The Three Sisters (above), towering remnants of an eroded sandstone plateau incised by rivers.

EASTERN RAINFORESTS

The Gondwana Rainforests of Australia World Heritage Area stretches from the rugged valleys and subalpine mountains of Barrington Tops NP (top right and bottom right), three hours drive north of Sydney, to southern Queensland. It includes 1156m-high Mt Warning, or Wollumbin (far right), in the far north east of NSW. Rich birdlife shelters in the forests, including regent bowerbirds (above left) and the superb lyrebird (above), the best avian vocal mimic in the world.

HIGH COUNTRY

Home to snow-blanketed ranges, mist-filled forests and gin-clear creeks that bubble down valleys, the High Country of southern NSW and the ACT is a region of dramatically changing moods. Visitors fly-fish for trout on sparkling waterways such as Swampy Plain River at Geehi Flats (above), cross-country ski across vast back country to high peaks such as Watsons Crags (middle top) or encounter wild brumbies (far right), the legendary feral horses that inhabit alpine areas. Local communities are small but active, enjoying a variety of year-round sports, such as mountain-biking and hiking when the skiing season finishes. The Lake Jindabyne Yabbies (middle bottom) brave the chilly waters of Lake Jindabyne. The swimming club was formed in the mid-1990s.

COASTAL BEAUTY

Like a priceless necklace, NSW's curvaceous coastline links emerald, sapphire and jade jewels along its 2007km length. The Sea Cliff Bridge (far left, top), opened under the Illawarra escarpment in 2005, rivals Victoria's Great Ocean Road for coastal driving pleasure. At Byron Bay (middle top), dedicated surfers surface at dawn and ride every accessible break until dusk. Home to one of the few remaining shack communities, Little Garie Beach in the Royal NP south of Sydney (left bottom), boasts 20 of the now heritage-listed buildings. On the northern outskirts of Sydney, Scotland Island and Pittwater estuary (above) are a water lover's paradise. The locality is heavily occupied, as is about 25 per cent of the NSW foreshore.

OUTBACK NSW

Beyond the Great Dividing Range, NSW's vast interior holds productive farming country, strong communities, rugged landscapes and characters galore. In the far north-west of the state, relics in the Golden Gully mining heritage site (far left) near Tibooburra speak of ages past. At Silverton, near the mining centre of Broken Hill, artist Peter Browne has painted emu caricatures on abandoned Volkswagen Beetles (opposite top). Wedge-tailed eagles (opposite bottom) are one of the most regularly seen outback bush characters, perched on fences and signs, or soaring high above. They have the largest wingspan of any bird in Australia, up to 2.8m. North-east of Broken Hill, Little Half Dome glows at Mutawintji NP (above left), and south-east of the town, Lake Pamamaroo (left) forms part of the Menindee Lakes oasis. Water in the inland acts like a magnet to animals, such as this royal spoonbill (above) near Lake Narran, in the north of the state.

CANBERRA AND THE ACT

Capital country of snow-capped ranges, granite cliffs and grasslands abounding in eastern grey kangaroos, the ACT is primarily made up of one national park – Namadgi (middle bottom). The historic park includes Aboriginal shelters, the remains of space-tracking stations used for Apollo missions, such as the first moon landing and old pastoral lands (above). Canberra, founded as Australia's capital in 1913, is home to many of our national collections and institutions, including Parliament House (middle top), with its forecourt mosaic designed by indigenous artist Michael Nelson Jagamara, and the Australian War Memorial with its Roll of Honour (far left, bottom). In March, balloons take off from Parliament lawn in the annual Canberra Festival (far left, top).

Dawn breaks in the capital, and pale pink mist swirls around the National Carillon (opposite left) on a spectacularly moody morn. Lake Burley Griffin, an 11km-long lake created in 1963 and named after the American designer of the city, Walter Burley Griffin, provides the watery foreground for many of Canberra's key features, including the telecommunications tower on Black Mountain (opposite right). A 36km cycling track goes all the way around the lake, past the modern National Museum of Australia (left), built in 2001. Being a completely planned and designed city, Canberra has many geometrical views, with major monuments and institutions lining up on axes. For example, the Australian War Memorial (above, in foreground), lines up with Old Parliament House and the current Parliament House behind it, with its 81m flagpole. In autumn, the combination of the ACT's sharp cold and many introduced trees, results in a colourful display in the city and on Brindabella station (above left), snuggled below the flanks of Namadgi NP.

AUSTRALIA'S SOUTHERNMOST mainland state is rich in natural beauty as well as contrasts. Cool, temperate forests and snow-capped mountains can give way to scorching summer heat and the occasional raging bushfire. And while the coastline is famous for its beaches and rock formations hewn by the southern seas, the north-west of the state features open wheatfields and semi arid desert.

Victoria was founded largely on the riches of gold. In the mid-19th century, diggers from around the globe arrived in droves to try their luck. Many left (or stayed) empty-handed, but towns such as Ballarat and Bendigo still retain glorious architecture from the era.

Melbourne is the capital city and it too basks in Victorian splendour with wide boulevards, leafy parks and grandiose buildings dating back 150 years.

Melbourne's other shrines – the Melbourne Cricket Ground and Flemington Racecourse – are the spiritual homes to Australian Rules football, the national cricket obsession and the Melbourne Cup.

Natural wonders abound out of town, from the wild and scenic Great Ocean Road in the south-west to the Victorian Alps in the north-east, and the verdant Dandenong Ranges in Melbourne's backyard. There are the Grampians ranges rising from the western plains, the mighty Murray River in the north, boundless tracts of forest in the east and scores of sleepy country towns and vibrant coastal communities in-between. Victoria's history, landscapes, quiet villages and cosmopolitan Melbourne are intriguing to visit, and its comparatively small land area means it is relatively easy to encounter the best of Victoria.

AROUND THE STATE

MORE THAN 4 MILLION Victorians call Melbourne home, but for all its size Melbourne is also known for its subdued charms, impressive Victorian architecture and the village-like atmosphere of its inner suburbs. Melburnians love their laneway cafes, restaurants, shopping, gardens and sport, as well as escaping to the beaches and wineries of the nearby Mornington Peninsula.

One of Australia's top destinations for overseas visitors, the Great Ocean Road clings tenaciously to Victoria's south-western coastline, winding sinuously between the tree-covered Otway Ranges and the crashing surf of the Southern Ocean. Quiet coastal villages such as Lorne and Apollo Bay swell with sun-seekers during summer, while quiet coves and the spectacular Twelve Apostles are destinations in themselves.

Victoria shares its alpine region with neighbouring NSW, and while its mountains might be low by world standards, they are dotted with ski resorts at Mt Hotham, Mt Buller and Falls Creek. There's the opportunity for walking and cycling in warmer months, and a multitude of small towns are home to boutique wine and gourmet producers.

In the state's east is Gippsland, a vast rural area of farms, bushland, lakes and beaches that is as surprising for its variety of landscapes as it is for its welcoming small towns. Whether it's boating, fishing or swimming in the lakes, or simply meandering through the hills looking for the next cheese producer, micro-brewery or winery, there is always something to do. In the south-east, Wilsons Promontory is a narrow-necked peninsula given over entirely to national park. It abounds in walking tracks, wildlife, mountains and magnificent beaches making 'The Prom' a natural wonderland.

The Murray is Australia's longest river, flowing some 2500km from mountains in the east, heading westwards through dry inland plains and eventually to the sea. It cuts through the quaint, river-port paddle-steamer town of Echuca and past the semi-arid Murray-Sunset National Park. In the state's west is the Grampians National Park with its rocky spires and bushwalking opportunities.

Pictured left: Yarra Glen in the Yarra Valley.

AROUND VICTORIA

Opposite page, clockwise from top left: Melbourne Cricket Ground and CBD; a restored paddle-steamer plies its trade along the Murray River at Echuca; a dozing koala; golden mist enshrouds the Yarra Valley; Norman Bay in the popular Wilsons Promontory NP; the World Heritage-listed Royal Exhibition Building; Centre Place, Melbourne; common heath, Victoria's floral emblem; bookies use betting indicator boards to display their odds in the Melbourne Cup.

This page, clockwise from top left: egrets and cormorants rest along the banks of the Murray River; Harvest Moon Festival, Bendigo; Mining Exchange, Ballarat; Yarrawonga Weir, on the Murray River; a fringed lily; All Saints Estate Winery in Rutherglen, northern Victoria; trawlers await their next voyage at Lakes Entrance in eastern Victoria; mist fills the tall gum forests in Great Otway NP.

GREAT OCEAN ROAD

Snaking alongside some of the most spectacular coastline in Australia, the Great Ocean Road passes forest, farmland and features of towering limestone at the mercy of the Southern Ocean. As waves crash into the cliffs of Port Campbell NP, they carve new forms: Island Arch collapsed in June 2009, leaving these two stand-alone islands (above). Similarly, in 1990, the double-arch of London Bridge lost the arch linking it to the mainland (opposite top), stranding tourists on the remaining structure. Amazingly no one was hurt. Nearby Great Otway NP is home to soaring mountain ash trees (opposite far left), the world's tallest flowering species, reaching more than 90m. Introduced radiata pines (opposite right) grow to about 50m in height.

ALPINE COUNTRY

With bustling ski fields, extensive back country, grazing land, pretty towns and alpine meadows that bloom with summer flowers, Victoria's alpine country is wondrous in any season. In Alpine NP, weathered snow gums encroach on the Davies Plain Drive (opposite top), a challenging four-wheel drive route that passes through a remote landscape punctuated with historic cattlemen's huts and sparkling mountain streams. The park is also home to the highest peaks in Victoria, including 1986m-high Mt Bogong and 1922m-high Mt Feathertop (opposite bottom). Nearby, the township of Bright (left), tucked into the Ovens Valley on the Great Alpine Road, becomes a kaleidoscope of colour in autumn. Round-topped billy buttons (above) add splashes of yellow to the high ranges in summer, along with other flowering alpine herbs and daisies, some of which are found nowhere else in the world.

MELBOURNE

With a reputation as Australia's cultural capital, Melbourne is home to Australia's largest capacity sporting venue, the 95,000-seat Melbourne Cricket Ground (opposite). First surveyed in 1861, the ground has seen many key sporting events including the 1956 Olympic Games, Ashes cricket matches and the annual Australian Rules football grand final. Architecturally, Melbourne is highly eclectic, with everything from the World Heritage-listed Royal Exhibition Building (middle), completed in 1880 and site of the opening of Australia's parliament in 1901, to ultra modern Federation Square (above) opened in 2002. St Kilda Pier (top) dates back to 1853. The breakwater, visible behind it, is home to a colony of about 100 little penguins.

EASTERN VICTORIA

Like splashes of paint, orange lichen festoons granite boulders (above) on Picnic Point in Wilsons Promontory NP, the most south-easterly area of mainland Australia. The region is well known for its rugged coastal features like those in Croajingolong NP (opposite far left), which occupies 100km of rocky coast, heathland and sandy stretches, and is home to about one-third of Australia's bird species. The Mitchell River, which rises in the Victorian high country, winds its way through vegetated silt banks that jut into Lake King (opposite top), while the Howe Range is just visible in the far distance beyond the turquoise waters of Mallacoota Inlet (opposite bottom).

WESTERN VICTORIA

In the west of the state, productive farmland, waterways and majestic mountains that rise above the plains slowly give way to the vast arid lands of central Australia. Abandoned plantation poplars (top) between Yarrawonga and Cobram once provided wood for match manufacturer Bryant & May. Boroka Lookout's lichen-spotted sandstone (left) catches the early morning sun in the Grampians NP (Gariwerd). A thick stand of river red gums crowds Sheet of Water (right), a pool that is filled when winter rains engorge the Glenelg River flood plain.

IN TASMANIA, CRUEL history is fast giving way to a cool future. The island's tumultuous history is on obvious show – from the convict stations at Port Arthur and Maria Island to the soft sandstone bridges that span its rivers, and the Georgian architecture that lines its streets.

Emerging from this history is a very different and very modern Tasmania, headlined by the likes of the boundary-pushing MONA art gallery, burrowed into a headland in Hobart's northern suburbs, a back-to-basics gourmet revival and a landscape that refuses to be tamed.

Australia's smallest state contains some of the country's greatest natural treasures. Framed by flour-soft beaches in the east, and surging Southern Ocean swells in the west, it's a tiny grab-bag of mountains, lakes, waterfalls, colourful cliffs, glacially carved valleys, sandy isthmuses, trout-filled rivers, lichen-smothered granite and tall towers of dolerite.

Raw wilderness is one of Tasmania's keystones – around 20 per cent of the state is designated as World Heritage Area, blanketing much of its western region. Vast areas of this remote and rugged area are inaccessible to all but the hardiest hikers and rafters.

There are places and natural features in Tasmania as familiar and evocative as any in the country. Port Arthur, Cradle Mountain, Wineglass Bay and the Franklin River are names that conjure up purity or hardship, or both. Squeezed into an area less than one-third the size of Victoria, Tasmania is the proverbial good thing in a small package.

AROUND THE STATE

EVEN IN HOBART geography is the defining feature, with the Tasmanian capital squeezed between the slopes of Mount Wellington and the banks of the Derwent River estuary. Founded in 1803 and home to around 215,000 people, it's Australia's second-oldest city, with one of the finest natural settings of any Australian capital. About an hour's drive from Hobart is the Tasman Peninsula, home to Australia's highest sea cliffs. It hangs onto the mainland only by the thread-thin Eaglehawk Neck isthmus. The narrowness of this neck made Australia's most notorious convict station, Port Arthur, almost escape-proof.

Tasmania's west is clad in almost 14,000sq.km of World Heritage mountains, forest and buttongrass plains, and is accessible in large parts only on foot. Iconic walking trails, such as the Port Davey and South Coast tracks, are the biggest drawcards to this literal wild west.

Road access opens up prime attractions elsewhere, such as the craggy summit of Cradle Mountain, the isolated fishing village of Strahan on the west coast and Australia's deepest lake, Lake St Clair.

Tasmania's east coast is a startling contrast to the west. Lined with beaches and small, low-key holiday towns, it's a colourful transition from land to Tasman Sea. Granite boulders are caked in vivid-orange lichen – such as at the appropriately named Bay of Fires – and, when the sun shines, the water is pure postcard brilliance. Hanging off the east coast is Freycinet Peninsula, with its musk-coloured Hazards, the mountain range that provides the dramatic backdrop to one of the state's signature scenes: the perfect curve of Wineglass Bay.

Tassie's second major city, Launceston, sits at the confluence of the North Esk and South Esk rivers – the latter burrowing through Cataract Gorge. The two rivers merge near the city centre to form the wide Tamar River, which flows towards Bass Strait through the vine-striped hills of Tasmania's major wine region.

Out in Bass Strait, the two largest islands – King and Flinders – form a pair of contrasting bookends. To the west, King Island's low-slung farmland yields some of Australia's finest specialty produce, while to the east Flinders Island is a visual masterpiece of empty beaches, abrupt mountains and prolific wildlife.

Pictured left: Coles Bay and the Hazards, Freycinet National Park.

AROUND TASMANIA

Opposite page, clockwise from top left: the sombre penitentiary on Masons Cove at Port Arthur; the Tasman Bridge, Hobart; view over Hobart from Mt Wellington; Painted Cliffs, Maria Island; Salamanca Place, Hobart, with Mt Wellington in the background; Horseshoe Falls, Mount Field NP; a common wombat; a white-bellied sea-eagle.

This page, clockwise from top left: Ketchum Bay in Southwest NP; Bennett's wallaby; stone bridge over the Coal River at Richmond, built by convicts in 1823; Kings Bridge across the Tamar River in Launceston; Tasmanian devil, the only surviving species of carnivorous marsupial; evening mist over Lake Oberon after a storm; the tiny leaves of 2m-tall fagus trees, or deciduous beech, turn golden in autumn; pied oystercatcher; the wild and woolly Scotts Peak in Southwest NP.

HOBART, PORT ARTHUR AND THE TASMAN PENINSULA

Port Arthur's museum and cafe building, seen here from the ruins of the hospital (far left), was built between 1864 and 1868 as an asylum to house and treat an ageing and increasingly infirm prison population in a more caring environment. Forty kilometres across the water, the Tasman Sea pounds at the rocky shoreline of Adventure Bay on south Bruny Island (opposite right). Fast becoming a cultural icon, MONA, or the Museum of Old and New Art, (above) in the northern Hobart suburb of Berriedale, attracted more than 600,000 visitors in its first 18 months of operation. The subterranean gallery showcases an extensive collection of ancient art, along with the ultra avant-garde, in a dramatic setting hewn from the sandstone banks of the Derwent.

THE TASMANIAN WILDERNESS

Australia's only native cold-climate deciduous tree, the fagus or deciduous beech (above), paints the shoreline of Lake Hanson in hues of yellow and gold, heralding the arrival of autumn on the Apple Isle. The plant, also known as tanglefoot, covers about 10,000ha mostly in the alpine zones of Mount Field and Cradle Mountain–Lake St Clair national parks. Cradle Mountain (opposite), with its characteristic jagged backbone perfectly reflected in Dove Lake's still, chill waters, is one of Tasmania's most popular sights and signals day one of the 80km Overland Track, a multi-day trek through some of Tasmania's most picturesque wild country. It attracts about 8000 walkers annually and takes around six days to complete. Peak walking season is November–April.

Moored in a tranquil dawn, a tinnie is secured to the beach of Forest Lagoon (above), an inlet off Bathurst Harbour in Southwest NP. Mt Rugby soars 772m into the clear blue skies above this remote region that achieved World Heritage status in 1982. In the park, the challenging South Coast Track traverses the tannin-stained waters of New River Lagoon (opposite top left). Walkers take 6–9 days to complete the 85km track. Alpine vegetation is dominated by pandani or endemic giant heath in the Anne Range (opposite right). Moss covers the buttresses of ancient myrtle-beech trees (opposite bottom left) in Cradle Mountain–Lake St Clair NP.

EAST COAST

The pure white arc of world-famous Wineglass Bay (above) draws photographers from far and wide to the Freycinet Peninsula on Tasmania's east coast. Most visitors view the beautiful bay from the Wineglass Bay Lookout, positioned in the saddle between Mt Amos, centre, and Mt Mason, disappearing to the left of the photo. The walk to the lookout is steep, but only takes one hour return. Fifty kilometres further south, sandstone swirls, circles and sculpted lines have formed another popular natural attraction: the Painted Cliffs of Maria Island (opposite). Once a penal settlement, the island is now a national park with no permanent human population, and abounds in wildlife, including kangaroos and wallabies, wombats and Cape Barren geese.

A trio of rock climbers (above) scales Whitewater Wall in Freycinet NP. Granite cliffs, beaches and boulders dominate the eastern Tassie coastline, such as at the legendary Bay of Fires (middle) in Mount William NP, in the north-east of the state. Birds are common on the coast, including Cape Barren geese, black swans, white-bellied sea-eagles, the endemic 40-spotted pardalote and the white-faced heron (far left).

WILD ISLANDS

North of the Bay of Fires coastline (above), sailors, kayakers, fishers and adventurers set out into Bass Strait towards a string of islands that were once the land bridge between Tasmania and the Australian mainland. In the Flinders Island group, Goose Island (opposite top left) offers refuge in its quiet bays and inlets. More than 300km to the west, King Island (opposite top right) is a gourmands delight, with renowned dairies, supplied by cows that occasionally dine on seaweed, and a thriving seafood industry (opposite bottom right). Back on the north coast of mainland Tasmania, at Table Cape near Wynyard, a patchwork of crops (opposite bottom) grows in the rich soil, including pyrethrum, a white daisy farmed for its insecticide oils.

FROM MALLEE SCRUB and gibber plains to blazing white salt lakes and spinifex-clad dunes, make no mistake – South Australia's interior can be a stark, forbidding place. And, on a summer morning when searing north winds blow into Adelaide, it feels like the desert is camped on your doorstep.

Yet the driest state in the land keeps tossing up surprises. With so many gulfs, islands and peninsulas, its shoreline is among the most richly faceted on the continent. Whatever the weather, there's a sheltered beach to wander or bay to fish.

By late autumn, the coast is another threshold for change as seasonal rains bustle inland from the Southern Ocean. Almost overnight, parched paddocks flaunt lush green growth. While grain and sheep farming are widespread, it's little wonder so many families arriving from southern Europe also revelled in this Mediterranean climate, farming a variety of produce.

From citrus groves to stone-fruit orchards and market gardens, sunny South Australia now has one of the most robust food cultures in the nation. It's also famed as home to Australia's premier wine regions. From the 1840s German immigrants helped pioneer grape growing in the Barossa Valley – and beyond.

Just as many of these original plantings endure as some of the world's oldest grapevines, so too do the traditions for marrying wine, food and art as an expression of place. In Adelaide, and in regions right across the state's settled areas, diverse communities come together to share these harvest blessings.

South Australians have a knack for organising festivals, both large and small. This is a state founded on the civilising ideals of freedom and social tolerance. In celebrating the good life the locals here uphold a history of innovation and the kind of hard-won respect for nature's gifts that comes from having the desert at your back.

AROUND THE STATE

TUCKED BETWEEN ITS gulf shores and the rambling Mount Lofty Ranges, Adelaide is arguably the nation's most liveable capital. The city's compact grid of streets and open squares is encircled by leafy parklands. There's an ease to life here; a convivial mix of work and business with art venues, markets, night-life and relaxed restaurants – all within walking distance.

When it comes to wildlife, Kangaroo Island has it all: from seals and penguins to wallabies, goannas, possums, echidnas, birds aplenty and, of course, kangaroos. It's one of the world's great nature strongholds. Add in a pristine coastline, beaches and a big-hearted community of farmers, fishermen and artists, and you have an island chock-full of treasures.

Like dinosaur backbones, the bumpy ridges of the Flinders Ranges stretch inland for nearly 400km. The ancient home to the Adnyamathanha people, this is terrain that's made for travelling. Even from afar the craggy sandstone peaks rise dramatically from the saltbush plains. The colour palette – stone in myriad ochre hues set against vivid blue skies – has always captivated artists and photographers.

Though seemingly timeless and unchanging, this landscape is dramatically affected every few years by big summer rains. Nowhere is this transformation more dramatic than Lake Eyre. As the dunes bloom and the waters flood in, so the lake becomes a miracle of desert life.

Flanked by huge river red gums and peaceful backwaters, the River Murray – as it's called west of the SA–Victoria border – has been South Australia's salvation. It's not just the towns, orchards and farms dotting its banks that thrive on the Murray. For Adelaide and rain-scarce communities as far afield as Whyalla, pipelines from 'the river' have brought life-giving flows. For many South Australians, the Murray also nurtures the spirit, as a place to camp and canoe, or kick back on a houseboat to cruise and enjoy the birdlife. And nowhere is this serenity more inviting than at the river's final hurrah – the sublime wetlands and dreamy, light-filled lagoons of the Coorong.

Pictured left: flat sheep country near Hawker, 370km north of Adelaide.

AROUND SOUTH AUSTRALIA

Opposite page, clockwise from top left: the Torrens River slicing through Adelaide; Cecil and Lachlan Brady at Cave Hill (Walinynga) in northern SA; Sturt's desert pea, the state floral emblem; Cooper Creek in flood; the curved pink granite shapes of Murphys Haystacks near Point Labatt; Bunyeroo Valley Scenic Drive in the Flinders Ranges with Mt Sawtooth in the background; zebra finches at Lake Eyre; emus; some of SA's abundant vineyards.

This page, clockwise from top left: pelicans in The Coorong; the number one outback accessory, an Akubra hat; windmill on the Hawker Plain; a yellow-footed rock-wallaby; Australian sea lions frolic off Point Labatt; Wilpena Pound, Flinders Ranges NP; a 7cm-long Lake Eyre dragon; camels and horses grazing together at Marree; anglers on Kangaroo Island.

KANGAROO ISLAND AND THE BIGHT

Melaleuca trees perch on the limestone headland at Shellgrit Beach (opposite top left) in the 150ha Pelican Lagoon Conservation Park at the eastern end of Kangaroo Island. With cliffs that plunge into a raging swell (opposite top right), the 4416sq.km island is a wildlife fortress, free of common pests such as foxes. Relentless ocean winds have sculpted the sandstone promontory of Kirkpatrick Point into Remarkable Rocks (opposite bottom left). Baird Bay, on the west coast of the Eyre Peninsula, is home to a colony of Australian sea lions (opposite bottom right). Further west, powerful swells pound at the limestone ramparts of the Bunda Cliffs (above) in Nullarbor NP.

FLINDERS RANGES

Within this "chain of rugged mountains", as explorer Matthew Flinders described them, lie "the bones of nature laid bare", according to early 20th-century painter Hans Heysen, who captured their beauty in watercolours. The Yourambulla Caves (above) preserve a wealth of much older Aboriginal paintings. River red gums (top middle) and yellow-footed rock-wallabies (top right) number among nature's riches here, while plants cling defiantly to a windswept red dune, west of the Flinders Ranges (bottom). The saw-toothed ramparts of Wilpena Pound (opposite) define the Flinders Ranges for many. Located 430km north of Adelaide, the pound lies at the southern end of the northern Flinders Ranges and forms a natural amphitheatre covering approximately 8000ha. It is a huge flat plain surrounded by jagged hills. The highest peak here is 1168m St Mary.

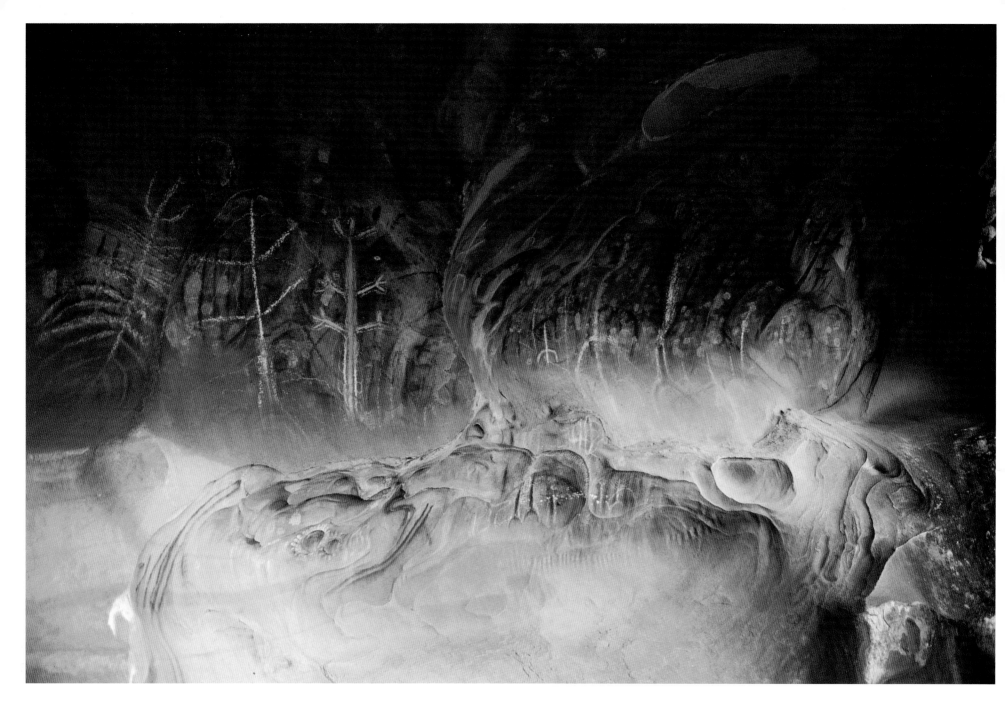

Wilpena Pound is a place of enormous sacred significance to the Adnyamathanha people who know it as Ikara. The rock art gallery at Arkaroo Rock (opposite) was discovered in 1959 during the search for a missing boy. Carbon dating suggests that Aboriginal people have been coming to the rock for 15,000 years. Built during the 1950s to supply water to the coal mining township of Leigh Creek, Aroona Dam (above) now forms part of a wildlife refuge for yellow-footed rock-wallabies.

LAKE EYRE AND THE DESERTS

Containing some of Australia's harshest but most starkly beautiful country, the arid lands of SA stretch out in all directions from marginal farmlands, where crops grow around abandoned buildings such as this one (opposite) at Burra, 150km north of Adelaide. In the centre of SA, miners search incessantly for opal around The Breakaways (top) at Coober Pedy. Water is highly ephemeral in most places out here, and even the salt-encrusted surface of Lake Eyre (left), which is slightly below sea level, receives inflows from Queensland rivers and floods once a decade, attracting huge flocks of birds, including banded stilts and silver gulls (above).

THE MURRAY RIVER AND THE COORONG

Majestically stitching two states together before carving through south-east SA on its way to the sea, the Murray River has broad, sweeping curves around Whirlpool Corner at Renmark (above). Countless river red gums drink their fill along the river, such as at the mouth of Banrock Creek, Banrock station, near Kingston-on-Murray (opposite top). Having drained one-seventh of the Australian landmass, and supplied essential water to much of Australia's most productive farmland on the way, the Murray finally spills into The Coorong (opposite bottom), where fishermen ply their trade in the brackish waters of this vast wetland ecosystem that comprises freshwater lakes, a saline estuary and lagoon and a 140km ocean beach.

WITH A LANDMASS of more than 2.5 million sq.km, Western Australia contains far greater diversity than most give it credit for. Its south-western corner is forested with some of the tallest trees on the planet, scraping the sky at up to 90m tall, while its northern tip harbours billion-year-old rock formations in glowing ochre hues.

Look hard and you'll see crevices marked with ancient rock paintings, created tens of thousands of years ago by ancestors of the world's oldest living indigenous cultures. The state's coastline wraps around one-third of Australia, and the crystal-clear ocean and fringing reefs that meet it act as a haven for endangered sea turtles and rare whale sharks.

In the cooler zones, there are hectares of vineyards with glittering estate names planted between strips of slender karri trees, while in warmer parts, rows of pearl-producing oyster beds are fed by giant tides, and waterfalls froth over worn rocks, like champagne bursting from a bottle. Meanwhile, just inland, vast reserves of minerals and resources are being dug up to sate the ravenous appetite of the world's expanding economies.

Often regarded as frontier folk – and long imbued with a boom or bust mentality – the state's population seems overly endowed with entrepreneurial spirit, producing more self-made millionaires than anywhere else in Australia. Western Australia's remote status is no longer holding it back and it is better connected in many ways with Asia than Sydney is. As recognition of its hefty earning power grows, and the need to prove itself to the rest of the country lessens, Western Australia is maturing, softening its new-money glitz and adopting a more statesman-like demeanour, albeit one sporting a flashy gold watch.

AROUND THE STATE

ONE OF THE world's most isolated cities, Perth is endowed with more sunny days than any other capital in Australia, and the calibre of its beaches matches the climate. Its outdoorsy residents, nicknamed 'sandgropers', frequently flee to car-free Rottnest Island, 19km off the coast, or claim their culture hit at boho haven, Fremantle.

Vast, ancient, and mostly undiscovered, the Kimberley is as rugged as it is remote. Bigger than Japan, it hosts remarkable landforms, most notably the huge orange and black-banded domes known as the Bungle Bungles in Purnululu National Park. Their beauty is a just reward for the effort involved in visiting. In the region's west, vibrant, multicultural and laid-back Broome maintains a constant holiday pace with its pancake-flat ocean, lazy beach strolls and sunset camel rides. But it's a different scene further south, where the mine-pocked landscape of the Pilbara seems to maintain a constant hum of industrial activity.

The region's deep red, iron-ore-infused earth contrasts sharply with its kingfisher-blue ocean, and a mix of island archipelagos, palm-fringed gorges and rock-art sites show there is beauty among the development.

Halfway up the western coastline at Shark Bay, bottlenose dolphins frolic in turquoise waters, drawing swooning tourists.

Nearby is one of the world's great wonders: a bed of stromatolites. Believed to be the oldest organisms on the planet, the fossils form a direct link to life forms that existed 3.5 billion years ago. Resembling small, squat stumps and growing only 1mm a year, they are regarded as major, fascinating signposts of our earth's evolutionary progression.

Western Australia's southern tip is blessed with more than its fair share of environmental wow factor. A hike along the Cape to Cape walking track between capes Leeuwin and Naturaliste reveals plenty: from fragrant bush trails flecked with a confetti of wildflowers and sun-dappled karri forests to limestone ridges edging the Indian Ocean where whales can be glimpsed on their annual migration.

The sea breeze tickles nearby vineyards that form a patchwork across the famous Margaret River region. It is the poster girl of the West Australian wine industry, its name synonymous with bottled excellence.

Further south at Albany, a more ruthless ocean pounds rock formations into interesting shapes, creating bridges, boulders and blow holes. A few hours east, past isolated Esperance, Cape Le Grand National Park offers coastal wilderness alongside blindingly white beaches. Scientific testing suggests the park's aptly named Lucky Bay has the country's whitest sand, and kangaroos are often spotted sprawling on it.

Heading back inland, home to Australia's largest open-cut gold mine, Kalgoorlie embodies the fervour, optimism and determination that comes with chasing fortunes. A mining town since the 1890s, a quarter of Kalgoorlie's working population is employed by the sector. Famous for its high proportion of pubs and the skimpily clothed waitresses that work them, it's an outback hub saturated with character. It's also the gateway to that most iconic of Aussie road trips, traversing the eternal flatness of the Nullarbor Desert along the Eyre Highway into South Australia.

Pictured left: in Joffre Gorge in Karijini National Park, the power of water erosion can clearly be seen in the sculpted cliffs.

AROUND WESTERN AUSTRALIA

Opposite page, clockwise from top left: Perth sits on the Swan River; the Mount Charlotte poppet head, Kalgoorlie; boab trees in the sunset at Derby; karri trees in the south-west forests; a pair of brolgas; a quokka, the small wallaby-like creature that inhabits Rottnest Island; a sheltered inlet at Elephant Rocks in William Bay NP, west of Albany; stromatolites, some of the world's oldest existing life forms; the 'Kings Park Special' bottlebrush. This page, clockwise from top left: a knob-tailed gecko; yachts sail past Esperance; Margaret River vineyards; the state faunal emblem, the numbat, which eats only termites; a green turtle at Ningaloo Reef; a camel train on Cable Beach, Broome; a western pygmy-possum on a mallee bloom; the exquisite and fragile Bungle Bungle formations in Purnululu NP; rippled dunes in the Delisser sandhills, Eucla NP.

THE KIMBERLEY

Land of many colours, the Kimberley glows like blood oranges at times, offsetting its vivid blue skies and milky seas. After the wet season in the east Kimberley, the spectacular orange and black Bungle Bungle formations (opposite) of Purnululu NP are accentuated by bright green spinifex. Over near Broome in the west Kimberley, glorious pindan cliffs at Gantheaume Point (above right) and Cape Leveque (above left) catch the sunset, and sailing ships (above top) cruise off Cable Beach. Hidden on rock surfaces throughout this region are many ancient paintings. The Bradshaw or Gwion Gwion figures (above centre) may be tens of thousands of years old – so old that they are now stains on the rock, and the original pigments that were used cannot be ascertained.

THE PILBARA AND BEYOND

With deep gorges, long stretches of quiet coastline, reflective pools and fascinating geological features, the resource-rich Pilbara surprises with sharp contrasts. A lone angler fishes in Murlamunyjunha (Crossing) Pool in Millstream–Chichester NP (top). The stunning recesses of Hancock Gorge in Karijini NP (right) are a just reward for adventurous bushwalkers. Shark Bay (above) is best known for the wild dolphins that choose to swim in the shallows to interact with people. Further north, Coral Bay (opposite bottom right) and Yardie Creek, in Cape Range NP (opposite top), display a treasure chest of jewel colours. In Nambung NP, (opposite bottom left) closer to Perth, thousands of limestone pillars, The Pinnacles, stand eerily on stark yellow dunes (middle bottom).

THE SOUTH-WEST

Although the most heavily populated part of WA, the south-west is still rife with wild and beautiful spots. The Indian and Southern oceans both smack into this corner of the country, providing awesome swells at places like Conto Beach (opposite top left) near Margaret River, and many places along the 135km Cape to Cape Track (above). Canal Rocks (opposite right), a day or so's walk on the track from Cape Naturaliste, can be a top snorkelling spot in calm weather, as can the clear waters around Busselton Jetty (opposite bottom left), which are alive with sponges, corals, seaweeds and fishes. Currently 1.8km long, the jetty, made out of karri, is one of the longest wooden jetties in the world. It has its own train and, at the end of the jetty, an underwater observatory.

Like a blanket of snow, a cloud drapes over Bluff Knoll in Stirling Ranges NP (opposite bottom left). Sitting at 1095m, Bluff Knoll is often subjected to wild weather and is one of the few places in WA to regularly receive snow. A classic 6km return walk goes to the summit and is renowned as one of the best in the area. Karri trees (centre), part of the eucalypt family, tower up to 80m in the south-west forests (above) with an annual rainfall of about 1200mm. As they mature, they shed their rough, dark, outer bark to reveal a smooth, fine-grained timber with light cream and pink hues that bring a lightness to the forest. Karri trees have a girth of up to 8m and have been logged extensively in the past. On Cape Naturaliste (opposite top left), wind-bashed melaleucas frame a calm day.

NATURE'S BOUNTY

Renowned in particular for its spring wildflower display, south-west WA is known as one of the world's biodiversity hot spots, with a high number of endemic species, including nearly 3000 plant species found nowhere else on earth, and six endemic threatened mammals. With an emphasis on the south-west, these pages show some of the many colours and creatures in this biologically diverse region of Australia's biggest state.

Opposite page: top row L-R: sticky eremaea; grass tree; honeysuckle; pink feather flowers; pixie mops.
Second row L-R: Mangles kangaroo paw, which is WA's floral emblem; grass tree flower; flame pea; red pokers and the prostrate and leafless *Leptosema aphyllum*.
Third row L-R: pixie mops; mottlecah; yellow pompom heads and golden everlastings; scarlet feather flowers; yellow feather flowers.

Fourth row L-R: native cornflower; coneflower; mottlecah; king spider orchid; sundew.
This page: big mallee blossoms (top left) provide bountiful nectar and pollen for the finger-length western pygmy-possum (top middle). The numbat (top right), however, eats only termites. The Goldfields bullfrog (bottom left) grows up to about 5cm and breeds in claypans after heavy summer rains in areas north and north-

east of Perth. Colourful Australian ringnecks (bottom middle) also known as twenty-eight parrots, are widely dispersed across the western half of the country, unlike the quokka (bottom right), which is now mainly restricted to Rottnest Island. The island was actually given the name Rottnest by 17th-century Dutch explorers who mistook the marsupial quokkas for giant rats.

The gorgeous granite, gneiss and sand coastline around Esperance is preserved in such national parks as Cape Le Grand (above). Walkers, joggers, campers and anglers enjoy its sheltered bays and coves. The park was named after a French explorer who sailed along this coastline in 1792. Golden crops near the Stirling Ranges NP (opposite left) are a darn sight easier to visually appreciate than the gold in the Wallaby ore deposit (opposite bottom right) at the Granny Smith Mine near Laverton. Much further west, near the border with South Australia, the Eucla Telegraph Station ruins (opposite top right) are being overrun by the windblown sands.

FROM THE SCREECH and cackle of the Territory's vocal birds at daybreak, backed up by the omnipresent chorus of cicadas, there's a sense that everything in the northern clime is excited to be alive. Nature's volume rises and falls with the tropical temperature, as fresh mornings morph into humid days followed by blood-red sunsets. The people – young, laid-back and imbued with outback character – relish the outdoors and are often found with a fishing rod in hand, cruising crocodile-infested waters with one eye on the liquid surface and another on the glittering horizon. They come from all corners of the globe, making Darwin a hotbed of multiculturalism, and add to the textures and layers created by the Territory's Aboriginal communities who have lived here for more than 50,000 years. All share a love of this wild and verdant land so transformed by the seasons.

Like yin and yang, the Territory's top and bottom halves are distinctly different; one steamy and green, the other dry, sandy and ochre stained. The Top End rallies in the Wet, with its gushing waterfalls, soaked wetlands and spectacular electric skies. Further south, the Red Centre responds to rare rains with carpets of colour, its desert grasses and wildflowers relishing the opportunity to shine. Both regions harbour World Heritage-listed wonders – think Kakadu and Uluṟu – and between them, tens of thousands of square kilometres have been protected, ensuring that nature roams free and ancient Aboriginal traditions can be maintained in the places they originated.

Accessible, authentic and awe inspiring, the Northern Territory is a region of extremes with a vibe like no other.

AROUND THE TERRITORY

IT MAY BE Australia's smallest capital city, but everything about tropical Darwin is larger than life. Its fun-loving, multicultural populous buzzes with upbeat energy – evident in its vibrant markets, bar-lined streets and on its harbour sunset cruises. Young at heart, residents are happiest outside, chasing adventures in the humid heat.

There's something magical about the light that shines over Kakadu. Nature awakens with sunrise's gentle illumination, and, as the temperature climbs, the region's lush, lotus lily-carpeted billabongs, its still, mirror-like streams and toothpick tree savannahs come alive.

The World Heritage-listed national park contains extraordinary diversity, with more than 280 bird species, over 2000 plant types, almost one-fifth of Australia's mammals and, of course, plenty of saltwater crocodiles embedded in its watery boundaries. Its history is as rich as its nature is abundant, with at least 50,000 years of Aboriginal stories painted onto its sacred rock formations, creating an important link to the descendants of today.

The heartbeat of indigenous culture thumps just as strongly in neighbouring Arnhem Land, which is entirely Aboriginal-owned.

Drier and rockier than Kakadu, Arnhem Land's towering escarpments contain countless natural art galleries known only to the local people. On the coast, faded orange earth gives way to albino beaches and crystalline waters where mud crabs are still expertly speared and barbecued.

A frontier town quite literally in the middle of Australia, Alice Springs, or simply 'Alice' to the locals, contrasts its dusty streets with the richness of its Aboriginal art galleries, the beauty of its surrounding ranges, the depth of its rural history and the diversity of its never-ending desert landscape.

As recognisable as the Sydney Opera House, majestic Uluṟu has a distinct presence drawn not only from its colossal size. Regarded as a sacred place by the local Aboriginal people, the 348m-high monolith, with a girth measuring 9.4km, hides age-old rock paintings in its ochre folds. Ayers Rock, as it's also known, plunges at least twice as far beneath the ground as it soars above the surrounding flat desert plains. Its dawn and dusk transformation draws people from around the globe who're eager to witness the fiery-red hues of its craggy surface as they bleed into deep, flat purples.

Equally mesmerising are the nearby domes of Kata Tjuṯa – unusual geological formations that sprout from the earth like high-rises burst from a city's core.

Closer to Alice Springs, the MacDonnell Ranges harbour deep chasms and watery gorges in metamorphic and igneous rock, providing welcome oases to the scorched surrounds.

Pictured left: 17 Mile Falls, along the 58km Jatbula Walking Trail that runs through Nitmiluk (Katherine Gorge) National Park.

AROUND THE NORTHERN TERRITORY

Opposite page, clockwise from top left: Mindil Beach Markets, Darwin; a ghost gum with the West MacDonnell Ranges behind; a carpet python coiled around a tree; a wedge-tailed eagle; storm clouds above farmland near the Stuart and Arnhem Land highways; newborn flatback turtles make a dash for the sea; a red horned sea starfish; a green tree frog; a saltwater crocodile; aerial view of Alice Springs; aerial view of Darwin; a Gouldian finch.

This page, clockwise from top left: freshwater rock pools at Gapuru, East Arnhem Land; a termite mound near the Roper River; dot painting; a frill-necked lizard; Nourlangie Rock, Kakadu NP; the Ghan train, which travels between Darwin and Adelaide; a woollybutt blossom; Uluru glowing vividly; competitors jostle for position during the 2011 Camel Cup at Alice Springs; the harmless, toy-like thorny devil.

THE TOP END

Water gushes over Jim Jim Falls (above), in the east of Kakadu NP. Millions of litres of water pour off the escarpment every minute in the Wet, but come the dry season, the waterfalls will slowly disappear and stop flowing altogether – sometimes as early as July. Like a writhing Rainbow Serpent, the mighty Adelaide River (opposite) switches back on itself as it gets closer to the sea. It is laden with brown silt that has been swept up by wet-season waters from overflowing flood plains and higher ground.

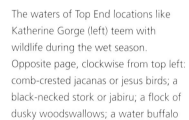

The waters of Top End locations like Katherine Gorge (left) teem with wildlife during the wet season. Opposite page, clockwise from top left: comb-crested jacanas or jesus birds; a black-necked stork or jabiru; a flock of dusky woodswallows; a water buffalo cools off in a billabong; Arnhem Land depictions of the Rainbow Serpent; the region's most feared predator, a saltwater crocodile.

This page, clockwise from top left: Fogg Dam, 50km south-east of Darwin, and its surrounds hold the highest known biomass of predator and prey of any ecosystem on earth, with thousands of 2–3m water pythons that feed on dusky rats. In a good season there are several hundred of the mostly nocturnal, olive-coloured snakes per hectare; darters, also known as snake birds, are commonly spotted roosting on bare branches along the edges of watercourses; lotus lily pads provide rich hunting grounds for jacanas and other waders; a flock of plumed whistling-ducks congregate at dusk.

In Australia's largest national park, the 20,000sq.km Kakadu NP, the prominent Nourlangie Rock massif (above and opposite top) sits imposingly beside the lush Anbangbang Billabong. A mecca for water monitors, agile wallabies, euros, egrets and other wildlife, it holds water right through the dry season (opposite bottom). Nourlangie is one of many prominent Aboriginal art sites in the park, with various styles represented in its 60 galleries, including X-ray art thousands of years old and paintings that show the arrival of Europeans. The main gallery focuses on a story about Namargon, the Lightning Man, a white figure with axes rising from his head, elbows and knees, who shakes the earth with lightning and thunder at the beginning of the wet season.

THE RED CENTRE

The geographical and spiritual heart of Australia is the Red Centre. It has wide arid plains broken up by jutting red rocks and a few surprising green gorges, such as Finke Gorge NP (opposite top left), the only home of the red cabbage palm. Behind stands of desert oak rise the red forms of Kata Tjuṯa (above). Composed of conglomerate, including granite and basalt, cemented by a matrix of sandstone, the 36 domes or bornhardts rise up above an otherwise flat expanse characterised by low-lying flora. There are plenty of other dramatic sights in the Red Centre, such as the mesas and jump-ups of the Finke River region (opposite bottom) and the extraordinary rounded granite boulders of Karlu Karlu, or the Devils Marbles (opposite top right).

At either end of the day the multicoloured sandstone of Rainbow Valley Conservation Reserve (above), a 100km drive from Alice Springs, displays an intoxicating desert palette. The red colouring comes from iron in the rock. The iron has been leached from the lighter coloured sandstone. A gnarled ghost gum (middle) catches the morning rays on Newhaven, a former cattle station, now managed by the Australian Wildlife Conservancy along with Birds Australia as a sanctuary. But perhaps the Territory's best-known feature for spectacular colour changes is Uluṟu. Its hulking sandstone form can be terracotta in the middle of the day (far right), but at dawn and dusk morphs miraculously through mauves, purples, pinks, oranges and reds.

ONE OF THE most naturally diverse places on earth, Australia's north-eastern corner is a medley of lush rainforest greens, brilliant coastal blues, bleached sandy ochres and rusty desert reds.

Bordered by almost 7000km of coastline and inland boundaries that reach for the heart of the country, Queensland is Australia's second-largest state. To its east, the Pacific Ocean and Coral Sea form a turquoise tapestry woven with atolls, cays and reef-fringed continental islands, where colourful coral ramparts teeming with marine life protect the coast from the ocean's crashing force.

Between sheltered coves and ragged headlands cloaked in ancient forests, a string of seaside towns spills onto sweeping, golden beaches. Emerald-coloured ranges cut by thundering falls and fast-flowing rivers rise from the coasts. Their steep-sided ravines brim with strangler figs and ferns, and their open woodlands roll into undulating farmland. Punctuated by towering volcanic crags and belts of granite boulders, these patchworks separate the Sunshine State's coast from its vast interior, where mobs of cattle graze on immense savannah tablelands. Historic outback towns pay homage to Queensland's golden pastoral age, and dusty flood plains rich with fossils recall an ancient inland sea. Clustered with grey-green spinifex, the sandy, scorched landscape stretches westward towards the terracotta dunes of the Simpson Desert.

Up north, Queensland's Gulf Country is marked by an ancient sandstone plateau where rugged red escarpments drop to palm-fringed creeks and lily-covered lagoons. However, it's in the far north that Queensland's wild side truly comes to the fore. Shaped by Wet-Dry cycles, Cape York Peninsula is an ever-changing landscape. Pocketed with rainforests, swamps and termite mound-studded grasslands, and traversed by corrugated highways that flood during monsoon rains, it is one of Australia's few remaining wilderness areas.

AROUND THE STATE

FLANKED BY HIGH-RISE buildings, the Brisbane River flows below the glinting skyline of Queensland's capital. Seething with sleek city ferries and spanned by the famous Story Bridge, the mangrove-lined waterway is the heart of the city. Moreton Bay figs sink their tangled buttress roots into its banks, and weatherboard Queenslanders perch on stilts in nearby suburbs, testament to the city's potential to flood. Mount Coot-tha stands sentinel over Brisbane, and from its 287m summit there's a northward view to the Glass House Mountains. These volcanic crags rise dramatically above the verdant farmland that separates Queensland's vast interior from the pandanus-fringed beaches and laid-back seaside towns of the Sunshine Coast.

Offshore lies the world's largest sand island. Fraser Island is home to giant dunes, towering rainforests and freshwater lakes. Life here is unhurried; a beach highway skirts coloured-sand cliffs and long stretches of surf, where manta rays flit above the waves. In contrast, the Gold Coast thrives on beach culture, glitz and glamour – high-rise apartments front onto golden sands lined with busy restaurants and bars.

The waters off the Queensland coast are home to the world's largest coral formation: the 2300km-long Great Barrier Reef. Teeming with tropical fish, sea turtles, manta rays, sharks, dolphins, dugongs and whales, the vivid corals and sponges form a colourful labyrinth beneath the crystal-clear Coral Sea.

The reef meets the rainforest at Cape Tribulation, in Daintree National Park. Here, the sea laps sweeping beaches and rocky headlands fringed with ancient rainforests, bringing two of the world's most unique protected areas together. Thundering falls and fast-flowing rivers cut through the deep-sided gorges of the Wet Tropics World Heritage Area, and forests brimming with strangler figs, bird's-nest ferns and orchids provide shelter for one of Australia's largest birds, the southern cassowary.

Further north, termite mounds stud the frontier country of the Cape York Peninsula. Clouds of red dust billow on the unsealed highways that connect isolated roadhouses during the Dry. Waterlogged rivers and creeks flood vast areas during the Wet, before shrinking into permanent waterholes that attract waterbirds.

Beneath big skies, the dusty plains of Queensland's vast backyard are etched with a serpentine network of oft-dry rivers. Rusty woolsheds, musterers' huts and stockyards – pastoral relics of an age-old agricultural tradition – pepper the baked landscapes of Matilda Country, the iconic home of the Australian swagman. Sandstone ridges, ochre-hued crags and semiarid cattle stations roll towards savannah-clad tablelands that eventually recede into the rust-coloured dunes of the Simpson Desert.

Pictured left: Mossman River, Daintree National Park.

AROUND QUEENSLAND

Opposite page, clockwise from top left: Brisbane's city skyline reflected in the waters of the Brisbane River; an emperor angelfish; South Molle Island in the Whitsundays; a school of brown sweetlips; 4WDs take to the world's largest sand island, Fraser; a southern cassowary, Australia's second-largest

bird; an echidna; a strangler fig; mulla mulla blooms; a northern fantail; surfers at Burleigh Heads against the jagged Gold Coast skyline.

This page, clockwise from top left: an azure kingfisher; Simpson Desert; a black kite; Pulchera Waterhole on the Mulligan River; a dingo; a perentie,

Australia's largest lizard species; Brahman cattle; the Country Women's Association hall, Cooktown; feral camels in the Simpson Desert; a hairy-footed dunnart; a cattleman's well-worn boots; a jackaroo looms through the bulldust during a cattle drive on Delta Downs station.

SOUTH-EASTERN QUEENSLAND

Known the world over for its beaches and holiday lifestyle, the Gold Coast (opposite bottom left) bustles with humanity. A morning walk on Surfers Paradise beach (opposite top left) is unlikely to be in solitude. However, just up the coast is the World Heritage-listed Fraser Island, where some of the purest dingoes in Australia pad the beaches (opposite top right). Mount Tibrogargan (opposite bottom right) is one of many peaks in the Glass House Mountains NP that are rhyolitic plugs formed by volcanic activity 25 million years ago. Granite Bay (above) is one of the northern-most beaches in Noosa NP, 150km north of Brisbane. The park is home to koalas and rare sedge frogs.

GREAT BARRIER REEF

Stretching for more than 2000km along Australia's north-east coast, the Great Barrier Reef is a resplendent chain of 2900 coral reefs and almost 1000 islands, home to more than 360 coral species, 1500 fish species, 1500 types of sponges, 500 different seaweeds and more than 200 species of bird. In the central section of the Great Barrier Reef Marine Park, the talcum-white beaches of Whitsunday Island (above) lure sailors and kayakers. Another 500km further north, near the popular holiday city of Cairns, visitors enjoy a sunset cruise (above top right). Because of the way light is absorbed by water, corals appear most colourful in the first metre or so (above bottom right) but even from the air (opposite) the amorphous shapes, colours and designs of reefs are exquisite.

Rich with life, the waters of the Great Barrier Reef delight snorkellers and divers, with everything from giant potato cod (opposite far left), which can grow up to 2m in length, to green turtles (middle), the most common of the six marine turtles found on the reef. Remarkably, green turtles usually return to the same place on the reef to sleep, often in a coral cave. Although young green turtles may eat small fish and crustaceans, they eat only seagrasses when adult, so this mixed school of fishes (above) is safe – from them at least. Of the 1500 or so fish species on the reef, more than one-third may inhabit only a single reef of 1ha. Together they provide a mesmerising kaleidoscope of moving colour, spinning and cascading around the corals.

THE RAINFOREST

Steamy, wet and lush, the tropical rainforests of the Daintree NP, 100km north of Cairns, extend down to sandy beaches in places. At Cape Tribulation, fan palms (above) grow up to 10m tall, their giant circular leaves sometimes reaching 1.5m across. The park is part of the Wet Tropics World Heritage Area, which contains some 2800 plant species, a quarter of which are endemic to the area. Some are ancient species with lineages that date back hundreds of millions of years. In another section of the park, the Mossman River (opposite left) burbles through a steep-sided gorge, tumbling over granite boulders and creating quiet pools fringed by mosses and epiphytes (opposite right), where jungle perch and even platypus may be seen if you linger long enough.

FAR NORTH

During the summer wet season, Barron Falls (above) becomes a tempestuous torrent as the river thunders off the Atherton Tableland through Barron Gorge NP near Kuranda. The force of the falling water is harnessed downstream at the Barron Gorge Hydro Power Station. Tidal retreat at Cape Tribulation leaves a red mangrove (opposite right) high and dry, its root tangle forming a three-dimensional maze. In the Torres Strait, Australia's most northerly islands, various indigenous communities keep their distinctive cultures alive, in particular through dances that are unique to each island. Here (opposite left) the Purple Spider dancers, in traditional attire with dari headdresses, dance on Darnley Island, more than 150km north-east of Cape York.

OUTBACK QUEENSLAND

In a cavernous entrance of the Undara Lava Tubes stands cattleman Gerry Collins (above), who opened up this tourist attraction on his family's property. There are 164 dormant volcanoes atop the Great Dividing Range near Cairns, and the most significant is the Undara volcano, which erupted 190,000 years ago. As the molten lava drained away, it left this tube system that extends for 100km. Much of outback Queenland is cattle country, with vast stations such as the 4500sq.km Delta Downs (opposite top left), north of Normanton. At dusk, dusty drovers (opposite bottom left) spin yarns, while a memorial to Banjo Paterson stands outside the Waltzing Matilda Centre in Winton (far right), the only museum in the world dedicated to a song.

MAP OF AUSTRALIA

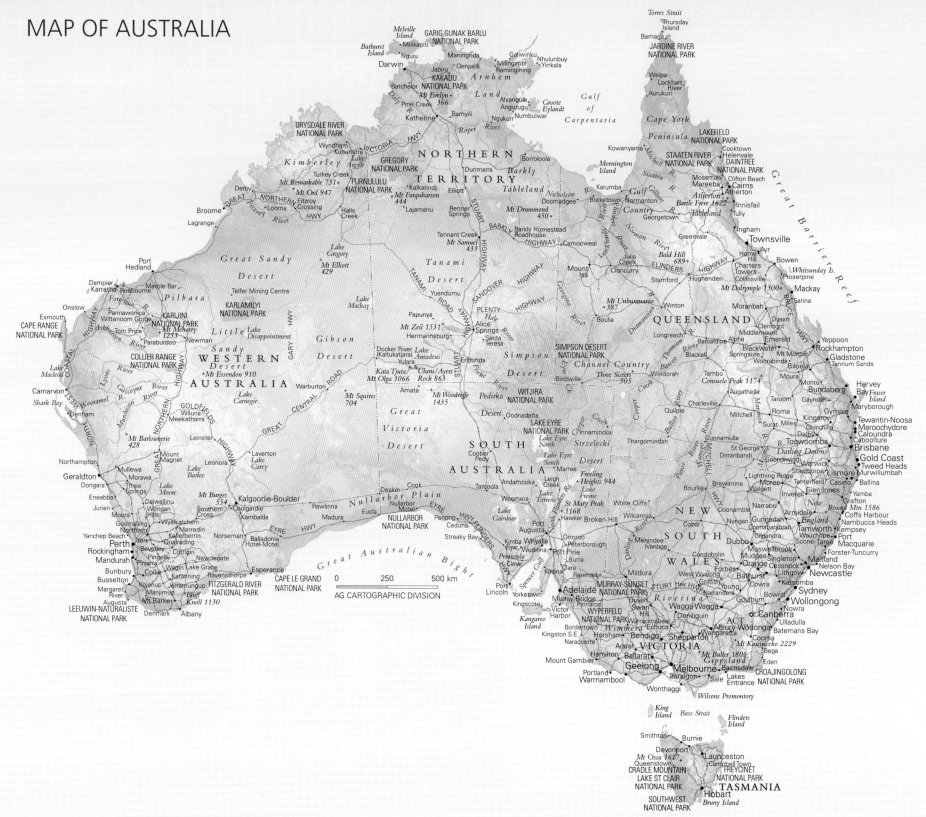

Following page: smooth-barked coolibahs stand in an ephemeral lake along the historic 1800km Canning Stock Route, WA.

Key
Page number is followed by page position.
R=right L=left T=top B=bottom
M=middle and combinations of these.

On montage pages, images are indicated numerically clockwise from top (1), (2) etc.

On page 88, rows are indicated by the letters a-e, and images numerically along each row, as in a1, a2, etc.

Frances **Andrijich** 78 (2), (Getty) 79 (6)

Auscape (Getty) 89 (TR)

Gonzalo **Azumendi** (Getty) 95 (10)

Bill **Bachman** 34 (2,7,8), 35 (1,4,6), 38 (T), 44 (B, T), 45, 60 (BR, BL), 64 (6), 65 (6,9), 66 (TL), 69, 74, 75 (T), 91 (BR), 95 (2,3), 99 (4)

John W. **Banagan** (Getty) 48 (3)

Allan **Baxter** (Getty) 34 (1)

Glenn **Beanland** (Getty) 34 (6)

Colin **Beard** 66 (BL)

Karl **Beath** (Getty) 13 (1)

Esther **Beaton** 12 (4), 25, 58 (R), 65 (4), 68 (TR), 103

Simon **Beedle** front cover (T, B), 36 (T), Back cover (T,M,B)

Melinda **Berge** 66 (TR)

Rob **Blakers** (Getty) 30 (L)

Nancy **Branston** (Getty) 108 (11)

David **Bristow** 35 (8), 78 (8), 83 (BL), 91 (TR), 110 (BL), 119

Hugh **Brown** 81 (BM)

John **Cancalosi** (Getty) 79 (4)

Leigh **Carmichael/Tourism Tasmania** 51

Brian **Cassey** 108 (6)

Katy **Clemmans** (Getty) 89 (4)

Tom **Cockrem** (Getty) 40 (BL)

Feargus **Cooney** (Getty) 76

Nick **Cubbin** 30 (R), 31 (TR), 31 (BL)

David **Dare Parker** 13 (7), 79 (2), 90, 94 (4)

Rodney **Dekker** 35 (2)

Grant **Dixon** (Getty) 49 (6), 54 (R)

Thien **Do** (Getty) 18 (L)

Hauke **Dressler** (Getty) 14

Jeffery **Drewitz,** 126

Tim **Dub** 50 (R)

Michael **Dunning** (Getty) 28 (BL)

Ross **Dunstan** 13 (9), 22, 23 (TL, R), 29, 31 (TL), 39 (R)

Paul **Dymond** (Getty) 94 (10)

Jason **Edwards** 49 (7), 52, 53, 94 (11)

Jamie **Evans** (Getty) 108 (1)

Warren **Field** 12 (7), 108 (9,10)

Cathy **Finch** 109 (7), 118 (L), 121 (BL)

Wayne **Fogden** (Getty) 34 (7)

Don **Fuchs** 12 (9), 35 (4,5,7), 42 (L, TR), 49 (2), 54 (TL), 60(TL), 88 (1a, 1b, 1c, 1d, 1e, 2a, 2b, 2c, 2d, 2e, 3a, 3b, 3c, 3d, 3e, 4b, 4c, 4d, 4e)

Lynn **Gail** (Getty) 95 (1)

STR/AFP/**Getty Images** 95(8)

Mike **Gillam** 102 (TL), 102 (B)

Chrissie **Goldrick** 12 (1), 37, 42 (BR), 48 (5)

Andrew **Gregory** front cover (M), 2-3, 13 (6), 20 (TR, TM, B), 24 (B), 27 (R), 61, 70, 79 (5), 83 (T, BR), 84 (TL, R), 85, 104, 106, 108 (3,11), 109 (1,5), 110 (TR), 117 (L, R), 118 (R, M), 210 (4)

Christopher **Groenhout** (Getty) 56

David **Hancock** 94 (1,3,5,7,12), 95 (4,5), 96, 97, 98 (TL, TR, MR, ML, BL, BR), 99 (1,2,3,5), 100 (T, B)

David **Hannah** 40 (TL)

Peter **Harrison** (Getty) 24 (TL)

Bill **Hatcher** 13 (10), 26 (TR), 27 (BL), 48 (6), 78 (4), 86 (R), 87, 89 (5)

Phillip **Hayson** (Getty) 84 (BL)

Shayne **Hill** (Getty) 78 (6)

Rodney **Hyett** (Getty) 24 (TR)

Richard **I'Anson** (Getty) 18 (R), 41

Image Source (Getty) 13 (3)

Darren **Jew** 65 (5), 66 (BR)

Anthony **Johnson** (Getty) 113

Warwick **Kent** (G) 17 (T)

Julian **Kingma** 34 (9)

Mike **Langford** 62, 64 (8), 65 (1,2,3,8), 68 (TM, BR, L), 70, 71

Randy **Larcombe** 75 (B)

Mike **Leonard** 34 (3)

Holger **Leue** (Getty) 112 (L)

Jiri **Lochman** 79 (1,7), 88 (4a), 89 (1,2,6), 94 (6)

Vincent **Long** 73 (TR)

Grahame **McConnell** 13 (4)

James **McCormack** 72

Mike **McCoy** 108 (2), 109 (8), 112 (TR)

Peter **McNeill** 28 (BR), 55

Chris **Mellor** (Getty) 64 (1)

Ray **Messner** 35 (3)

David **Messent** (Getty) 16, 28 (TL)

Bruce **Miller** 48 (4)

Alex **Misiewicz** (Getty) 112 (BR)

Frances **Mocnik** 12 (2), 23 (BL), 121 (R)

Stephan **Munday** (Getty) 15

Robbi **Newman** 12 (8)

Matthew **Newton** 48 (1), 50 (L)

Rob **Olver** 4-5, 91 (L)

Tim **Phillips** (Getty) 64 (9)

Chris **Pritchard** (Getty) 17 (B)

Neal **Pritchard** (Getty) 78 (1)

Yury **Prokopenko** (Getty) 28 (TR)

Tourism **Queensland** 111

Paul **Raffaele** 82 (BL)

Nick **Rains** 6-7, 20 (TL), 21, 46, 48 (8), 49 (8), 58 (L), 59, 64 (3,7), 73 (L, BR), 79 (8), 80, 82 (TL), 92, 95 (7), 108 (7), 109 (2,3,4,6,9,10)

Mitch **Reardon** 12 (6), 13 (5), 26 (L, BR) 64 (5), 67, 78 (5), 94 (8),

Douglas David **Seifert** 115 (L,R)

Barry **Skipsey** 13 (2), 64 (2), 81 (BL), 94 (2), 95 (3), 102 (TR), 104 (M)

Slow Images (Getty) 12 (5)

Dick **Smith** 64 (9)

Robin **Smith** (Getty) 48 (2)

Murray **Spence** 109 (11,12), 120, 121 (TL)

Mark **Spencer** 108 (4), 114 (L)

Bob **Stefko** (Getty) 86 (BL)

Oliver **Strewe** (Getty) 8-9, 12 (3)

Tourism **Tasmania** 51, 57

Steve **Turner** (Getty) 49 (5)

David **Wall** (Getty) 94 (11), 105 (R) 40 (R)

Rob **Walls** 60 (TR)

Peter **Walton** (Getty) 10, 13 (3), 19, 27 (TL), 32, 34 (4,5), 36 (BL, BR), 38 (B), 39 (L), 43, 48 (7), 49 (1,3,9), 54 (BL), 78 (3,7,9), 79 (3,9) 81 (TL, R), 86 (TL), 94 (9), 101, 110 (TL, BR), 116

Andrew **Watson** (Getty) 49 (4)

Thomas **Wielecki** 95 (6)

Steve **Wilson** 65 (7), 95 (9)

First published in 2013 by:

Bauer Media
54 Park Street, Sydney, NSW 2000
Telephone (02) 9263 9813, Fax (02) 9216 3731
Email editorial@ausgeo.com.au
www.australiangeographic.com.au

MEDIA GROUP

Australian Geographic customer service: 1300 555 176 (local call rate within Australia). From overseas +61 2 8667 5295

Editor Chrissie Goldrick

Writers

Introduction and South Australia introduction by Quentin Chester

NSW and ACT introduction by Elizabeth Ginis

Victoria introduction by Jenny Lamattina

Tasmania introduction by Andrew Bain

WA and NT introduction by Fleur Bainger

Queensland introduction by Joanna Egan

Picture captions by Ken Eastwood and Chrissie Goldrick

Picture research and editing Jessica Teideman, Maisie Keep

Prepress Mike Ellott, Filip Bartkowiak

Print production Chris Clear

Sub-editor Amy Russell

Cartography Dan Bowles

Proofreader Nina Paine

Managing Director Matthew Stanton

Publishing Director Gerry Reynolds

Associate Publisher, Specialist Division Jo Runciman

Book design by Trisha Garner, Design Patsy, Melbourne.

Printed in China by 1010 Printing Asia Limited, Suite 1b, 41 Park Road, Milton, QLD 4064.

MIX
Paper from
responsible sources
FSC® C016973

National Library of Australia Cataloguing-in-Publication entry

Title:	Postcards from Australia : a pictorial journey / edited by Chrissie Goldrick.
ISBN:	9781742454085 (hbk.)
Notes:	Includes index.
Subjects:	Australia--Pictorial works.
	Australia--Description and travel.
Dewey Number:	919.4